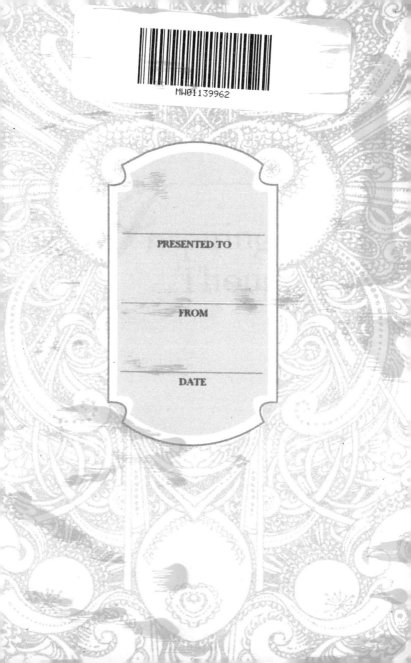

₹ 125

ISBN : 978-81-7028-926-5

Edition : 2014 © Rajpal & Sons

INSPIRING THOUGHTS OF SWAMI VIVEKANAND

Compiled by Meera Johri

Printed at Deepika Enterprises, Delhi

RAJPAL & SONS
1590, Madarsa Road, Kashmere Gate, Delhi-110006
Phone : 011-23869812, 23865483, Fax : 011-23867791
website : www.rajpalpublishing.com
e-mail : sales@rajpalpublishing.com

Inspiring
Thoughts

SWAMI VIVEKANAND

rajpal

*W*e are responsible for
what we are
And whatever we wish ourselves to
be
we have the power to make
ourselves
If what we are now
has been the result of our own
past actions
it certainly follows that whatever
we wish to be in future
can be produced by our present
actions
so we have to know how to act

*F*ill the brain with
high thoughts and highest ideals
place them day and night before
you
and out of that
will come great work

*W*e reap what we sow
We are the makers of our own fate
None else has the blame
None has the praise

*F*ear is death
Fear is sin
Fear is hell
Fear is unrighteousness
Fear is wrong life
All the negative thoughts and ideas
that are in the world
have proceeded from this
evil spirit of fear

*T*his is the first lesson to
learn
be determined not to curse
anything outside
not to lay the blame upon anyone
outside
but stand up
lay the blame on yourself
You will find that is always true
Get hold of yourself.

$\mathcal{I}$t is our own mental
attitude which
makes the world what it is for us
Our thoughts make things
beautiful
Our thoughts make things ugly
The whole world is
in our own minds
Learn to see things in the proper
light

*D*on't look back
only forward!
Infinite energy
infinite enthusiasm
infinite daring and
infinite patience
then alone can
great deeds be accomplished

Condemn none
If you can stretch out a helping
hand
do so
If you cannot
fold your hands
bless your brothers
and let them go their own way

$\mathcal{T}$his life is a hard fact
work your way through it boldly
though it may be adamantine
no matter, the soul is stronger

*D*esire, ignorance, and
inequality
this is the trinity of bondage

The world is the great
gymnasium
where we come to
make ourselves strong

You cannot believe in God
until
you believe in yourself

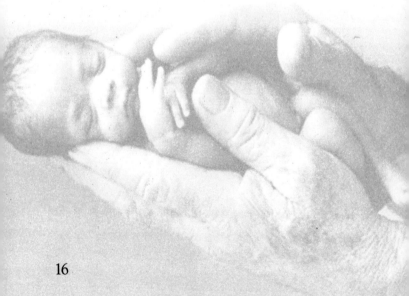

16

You have to grow from the
inside out
None can teach you
None can make you spiritual
There is no other teacher
but your own soul

$\mathcal{T}$ruth can be stated in
a thousand different ways
Yet each one
can be true

$\mathscr{A}$s different streams
having different sources
all mingle their waters in the sea
So different tendencies
various though they appear
crooked or straight
all lead to God

We are what our thoughts
have made us
So take care about what you think
Words are secondary
Thoughts live
they travel far

A few heart-whole
sincere and energetic
men and women
can do more in a year than
a mob in a century

*W*henever we attain a
higher vision
the lower vision disappears of itself

"Comfort" is no test of truth
on the contrary
Truth is often far from being
"comfortable"

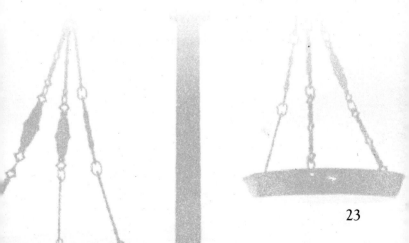

Those who grumble at the
little things
that has fallen to their lot to do
will grumble at everything
Always grumbling
they will lead a miserable life
But those who do their duty
putting their shoulder to the
wheel
will see the light and
higher and higher duties
will fall to their share

*A*re great things ever
done smoothly?
Time, patience, and indomitable
will must show

The world is ready to give
up its secrets
if we only know how to knock
how to give it the
necessary blow
The strength and force
of the blow
come through concentration

*W*ork and worship are
necessary
to take away the veil
to lift off
the bondage and illusion

Perfection does not come
from
belief or faith
Talk does not count for anything
Parrots can do that
Perfection comes through
selfless work

*K*nowledge can only be
got in one way
the way of experience
There is no other way to know

$\mathcal{S}$tand up for God
let the world go

*A*nything that brings
spiritual, mental, or physical
weakness
touch it not
with the toes of your feet

$\mathcal{B}$ooks are infinite in
number and time is short
The secret of knowledge is
to take what is essential
Take that and try to live up to it

*N*either seek nor avoid
Take what comes
It is liberty to be affected by
nothing
Do not merely endure
Be unattached

*I*n a day when you do not
come across any problems
you can be sure
that you are travelling
on the wrong path

When once you consider
an action
do not let anything dissuade you
Consult your heart
not others
and then
follow its dictates

All love is expansion
all selfishness is contraction
Love is therefore the only law of
life
He who loves
lives
he who is selfish
is dying
Therefore love
for love's sake
because it is
law of life
just as
you breathe to live

Each work has to pass
through these stages
ridicule
opposition
and then acceptance
Those who think
ahead of their time are
sure to be misunderstood

$\mathcal{T}$he only test of good
things is
that they make us strong

$\mathcal{E}$verything can be sacrificed
for truth
but truth cannot be sacrificed for
anything

Good motives
sincerity and
infinite love
can conquer the world
One single soul
possessed of these virtues
can destroy
the dark designs of millions of
hypocrites and brutes

All truth is eternal
Truth is nobody's property
No race
No individual
can lay any exclusive claim to it
Truth is the nature of all souls

*S*oft-brained people
weak-minded, chicken hearted
cannot find the truth
One has to be free
and as broad as the sky

The more we grow in
love, virtue and holiness
the more we see
love, virtue and holiness outside
All condemnation of others
really condemns ourselves
Adjust the microcosm
which is in your power to do
and the macrocosm will adjust
itself for you
It is like hydrostatic paradox
one drop of water
can balance the universe

What I want is muscles of
iron
and nerves of steel
inside which
dwells a mind of the same material
as that of which
the thunderbolt is made

*W*omen will work out their
destinies
much better than men can
ever do for them
All the mischief to women has
come
because men undertook to
shape the destiny of women

*T*ake up one idea
Make that one idea your life
Think of it
Dream of it
Live on that idea
Let the brain, muscles, nerves
every part of your body
be full of that idea
and just leave every other idea
alone
This is the way to success
that is the way great spiritual
giants are produced

*I*f you think about disaster
you will get it
Brood about death and
you hasten your demise
Think positively and masterfully
with confidence and faith
and life becomes more secure
more fraught with action
richer in achievement and
experience

*T*he greatest religion is to be
true to your own nature
Have faith in yourselves

To devote your life to
the good of all
and to
the happiness of all
is religion
Whatever you do for
your own sake
is not religion

The will is not free
it is a phenomenon bound by
cause and effect
but there is something behind the
will
which is free

*A*ll differences in this
world
are of degree
not of kind
because
oneness is the secret of
everything

*R*eligion is the
manifestation of
the Divinity already in man

$\mathcal{E}$xternal nature is
only internal nature writ large

$\mathcal{T}$ell the truth boldly
whether it hurts or not
Never pander to weakness
If truth is too much for
people and sweeps them away
let them go
the sooner the better

*F*ace the brutes
That is a lesson for all life
face the terrible
face it boldly
Like the monkeys
the hardships of life fall back
when we cease
to flee before them

I
for one
thoroughly believe
that no power in the universe
can withhold from anyone
anything they really deserve

The whole secret of
existence is
to have no fear
Never fear what will become of
you
depend on no-one
Only the moment you
reject all help
are you free

God is merciful to
those whom
He sees struggling heart and soul
for realization
But remain idle
without any struggle
and you will see
that His grace will never come

*G*reat work requires
great and persistent effort
for a long time
Character has to be established
through a thousand stumbles

*E*ven the greatest fool
can accomplish a task if
it were after his or her heart
But the intelligent ones
are those who can convert every
work
into one that suits their taste

$\mathcal{L}$earning and wisdom are
superfluities
the surface glitter merely
but it is the heart that
is the seat of all power

We are ever free if we
would only believe it
only have faith enough
You are the soul
free and eternal
ever free, ever blessed
Have faith enough and
you will be free in a minute

*I*f there is one word
that you find coming out like a
bomb
from the 'Upanishads'
bursting like a bombshell upon
masses of ignorance
it is the word "fearlessness"

The powers of the mind
should be concentrated
and the mind
turned back upon itself
as the darkest places reveal
their secrets
before the penetrating rays of the
sun
so will the concentrated mind
penetrate its own innermost
secrets

Come out into the broad light
of day
Come out from the little narrow
paths
For how can the infinite soul
rest content to live and die
in small ruts?

*S*uperstition is our great enemy
but bigotry is worse

66

*I*f you want to have life
you have to die every moment for
it
Life and death are only different
expressions of the same thing
Looked at from different
standpoints
they are the falling and the rising
of the same wave
and the two form one whole

*I*s there any sex-distinction
in the 'Atman' or Self?
Out with the differentiation
between man and woman all is
'Atman'!
Give up the identification with the
body and stand up!

*T*o succeed
you must have
tremendous perseverance
tremendous will
"I will drink the ocean
at my will
mountains will crumble up"
says
the persevering soul
Have that sort of energy
that sort of will
Work hard
and you will reach the goal

*A*bove all
beware of compromises
I do not mean that you are to
get into antagonism with anybody
but you have to hold on to your
own principles
in wealth or woe and
never adjust them to others' fads
through the greed of getting
supporters

*A*ll power is within you
You can do anything and
everything
Believe in that
Do not believe that
you are weak
do not believe that
you are half-crazy lunatics
as most of us do nowadays
Stand up and express
the divinity within you

$\mathcal{B}$rave, bold men and
women
these are what we want
What we want is
vigour in the blood
strength in the nerves
iron muscles and nerves of steel
not softening namby-pamby ideas
Avoid all these
Avoid all mystery
There is no mystery in religion

$\mathcal{B}$y doing well the duty
which
is nearest to us
the duty which
is in our hands now
we make ourselves stronger
and improving our strength
in this manner
step by step
we may reach a state
in which it shall be our privilege
to do the most coveted and
honoured
duties in life and in society

*D*o not look back upon
what has been done
Go ahead!

*Experience is the only teacher
we have
We may talk and reason all our
lives
but we shall not understand a
word of truth until
we experience it ourselves*

*G*ive up all desire for
enjoyment in earth or heaven
Control the organs of the senses
and control the mind
Bear every misery
without even knowing that you
are miserable
Think of nothing
but spiritual freedom

*I*f the mind is intensely
eager
everything can be accomplished
Mountains can be
crumbled into atoms

*I*f you want to be a 'Yogi'
you must be free
and place yourself in
circumstances where
you are alone and free from all
anxiety
One who desires a comfortable
and nice life
and at the same time
wants to realize the 'Atman'
is like the fool
who wanting to cross the river
caught hold of a crocodile
mistaking it for a log of wood

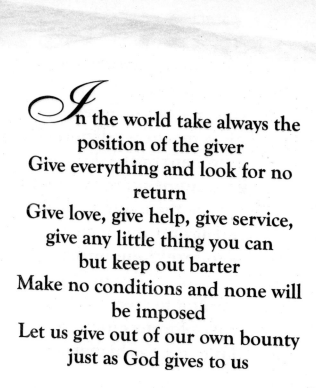

*I*n the world take always the
position of the giver
Give everything and look for no
return
Give love, give help, give service,
give any little thing you can
but keep out barter
Make no conditions and none will
be imposed
Let us give out of our own bounty
just as God gives to us

$\mathcal{I}$t is always for greater joy
that
you give up the lesser
This is practical religion
the attainment of freedom and
renunciation
Renounce the lower so that
you may get the higher
Renounce! Renounce!
Sacrifice! Give up!
Not for zero
Not for nothing
but to get the higher

It is only by doing good to
others
that one attains to one's own good

*I*t is only work that is done
as a free-will
offering to humanity and to
nature
that does not bring with it
any binding attachment

The happiest moments we
ever know
are when we entirely forget
ourselves

Let us make our hearts as big
as the ocean
to go beyond all the trifles of the
world
and see it only as a picture
we can then enjoy the world
without
being in anyway
affected by it

So long as there is desire or
want
it is a sure sign that
there is imperfection
A perfect, free being
cannot have any desire

Please everyone
without becoming
a hypocrite
or
a coward

*I*mpurity is a mere
superimposition
under which your real nature
has become hidden
But the real you is
already perfect
already strong

*I*n judging others
we always judge them
by our own ideals
That is not as it should be
Everyone must be judged
according to his own ideal
and not by that
of anyone else

*R*enunciation is the very
basis of our true life
Every moment of goodness and
real life that we enjoy is
when we do not think of ourselves

$\mathcal{Y}$ou must avoid excessive
merriment
A mind in that state never
becomes calm
it becomes fickle
Excessive merriment will always
be followed by sorrow
Tears and laughter are near kin
People so often run
from one extreme to the other

When an idea
exclusively occupies the mind
it is transformed into
an actual physical or mental state

*S*tand up
Be bold
Be strong
Take the whole responsibility on
your own shoulders
and know that you are the creator
of
your own destiny
All the strength and succour you
want
is within yourselves
Therefore
make your own future

Be a hero
Always say
I have no fear
Tell this to everyone
'Have no fear'

All knowledge
that the world has ever received
comes from the mind
The infinite library of the
universe
is in our own mind

Religion as a science
as a study
is the greatest and healthiest
exercise
that the human mind can have

Desire is the father of all
misery
Desires are bound
by the laws of
success and failure
Desires must bring misery
The great secret of true success
of true happiness
is this
the person who asks for no return
the perfectly unselfish person
is the most successful

$\mathcal{D}$o not hate anybody
because that hatred which comes
out from you
must, in the long run
come back to you
If you love
that love will come back to you
completing the circle

Freedom can never be
reached by the weak
Throw away all weakness
Tell your body that it is strong
Tell your mind that it is strong
And have unbounded faith and
hope in yourself

*H*old to the idea
"I am not the mind
I see that I am thinking
I am watching my mind act"
and each day the identification of
yourself
with thoughts and feelings will
grow less
until at last you can
entirely separate yourself from the
mind and
actually know it to be apart from
yourself

If you think that you are
bound
you remain bound
you make your own bondage
If you know that you are free
you are free this moment
This is knowledge
knowledge of freedom
Freedom is the goal of all nature

Oh, to live even for a day
in the full light of freedom
to breathe the free air of simplicity
Isn't that the highest purity?

Those who live for others
really live
and
those who live only for themselves
are more dead
than alive

*N*ever lose faith in
yourself
you can do anything in the
universe

It is the cheerful mind
that is preserving
It is the strong mind
that hews its way through a
thousand difficulties